TRUC

MW01148238

Year:	
Make:	
Model:	
Trim:	
VIN:	
Purchase Date:	
Miles:	
Owner Name:	
Address:	
Phone:	
Notes:	

Notes

PARTS AND FLUIDS

Air Filter:
Fuel Filter:
Oil Filter:
Oil Brand:
A.T. Fluid:
Transfer Case:
Axle Lube:
Headlight Bulb:
Turn Signals:
Taillight:
Notes:

Mark C=Check or R=Replace

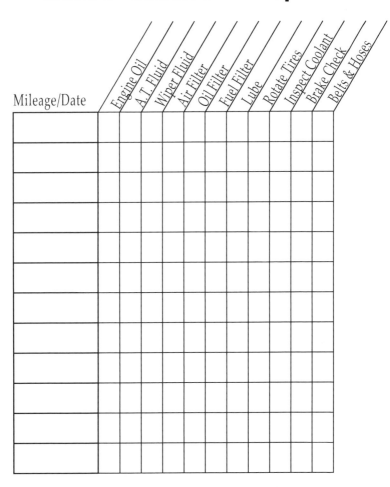

Mileage/Date	Engine Oil	A.T. Fluid	Wiper Fluid	Air Filter	Oil Filter	Fuel Filter	Lube	Rotate Tires	Inspect Coolant	Brake Check	Belts & Hoses

Note Repairs/Purchases

Mark C=Check or R=Replace

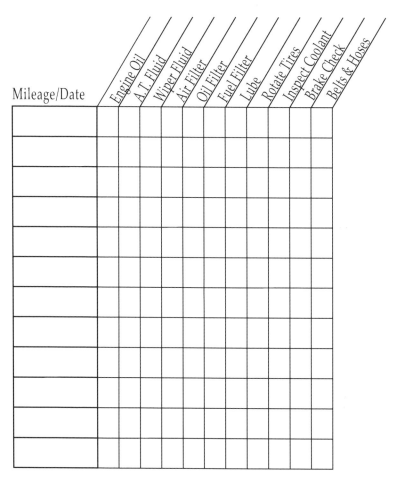

Mileage/Date	Engine Oil	A.T. Fluid	Wiper Fluid	Air Filter	Oil Filter	Fuel Filter	Lube	Rotate Tires	Inspect Coolant	Brake Check	Belts & Hoses

Note Repairs/Purchases

Mark C=Check or R=Replace

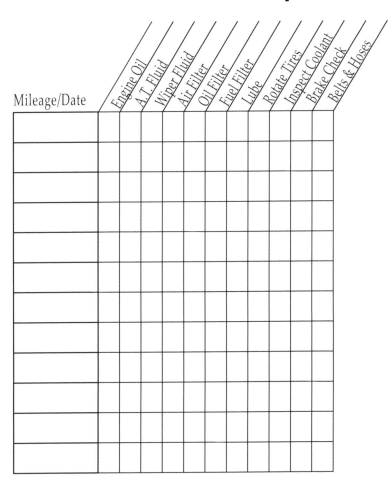

Mileage/Date	Engine Oil	A.T. Fluid	Wiper Fluid	Air Filter	Oil Filter	Fuel Filter	Lube	Rotate Tires	Inspect Coolant	Brake Check	Belts & Hoses

Note Repairs/Purchases

Mark C=Check or R=Replace

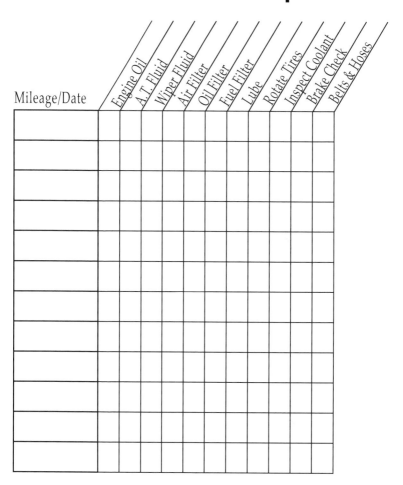

Mileage/Date	Engine Oil	A.T. Fluid	Wiper Fluid	Air Filter	Oil Filter	Fuel Filter	Lube	Rotate Tires	Inspect Coolant	Brake Check	Belts & Hoses

Note Repairs/Purchases

Mark C=Check or R=Replace

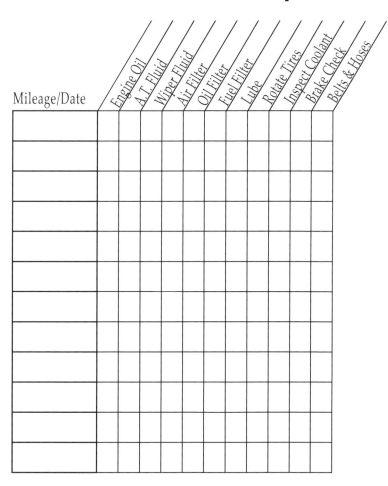

Mileage/Date	Engine Oil	A.T. Fluid	Wiper Fluid	Air Filter	Oil Filter	Fuel Filter	Lube	Rotate Tires	Inspect Coolant	Brake Check	Belts & Hoses

Note Repairs/Purchases

Mark C=Check or R=Replace

Mileage/Date	Engine Oil	A.T. Fluid	Wiper Fluid	Air Filter	Oil Filter	Fuel Filter	Lube	Rotate Tires	Inspect Coolant	Brake Check	Belts & Hoses

Note Repairs/Purchases

Mark C=Check or R=Replace

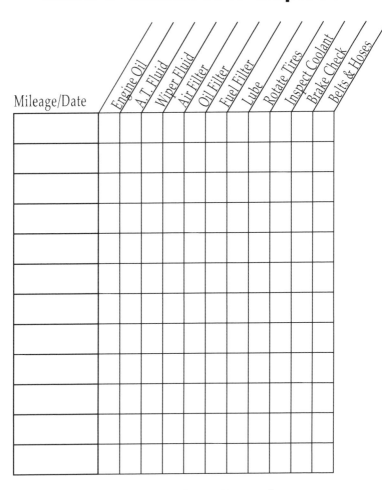

Mileage/Date	Engine Oil	A.T. Fluid	Wiper Fluid	Air Filter	Oil Filter	Fuel Filter	Lube	Rotate Tires	Inspect Coolant	Brake Check	Belts & Hoses

Note Repairs/Purchases

Mark C=Check or R=Replace

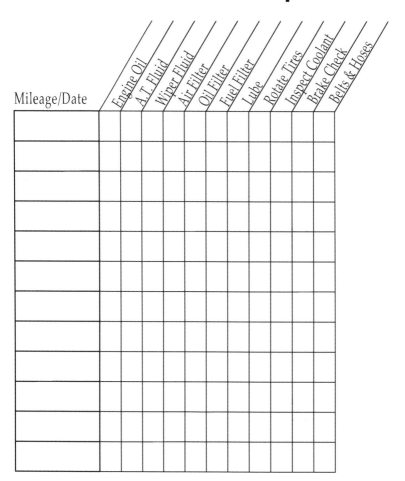

Mileage/Date	Engine Oil	A.T. Fluid	Wiper Fluid	Air Filter	Oil Filter	Fuel Filter	Lube	Rotate Tires	Inspect Coolant	Brake Check	Belts & Hoses

Note Repairs/Purchases

Mark C=Check or R=Replace

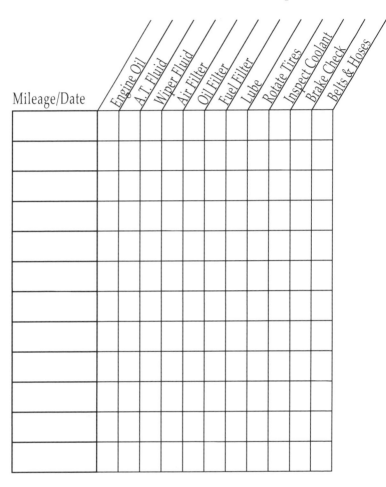

Mileage/Date	Engine Oil	A.T. Fluid	Wiper Fluid	Air Filter	Oil Filter	Fuel Filter	Lube	Rotate Tires	Inspect Coolant	Brake Check	Belts & Hoses

Note Repairs/Purchases

Mark C=Check or R=Replace

Mileage/Date	Engine Oil	A.T. Fluid	Wiper Fluid	Air Filter	Oil Filter	Fuel Filter	Lube	Rotate Tires	Inspect Coolant	Brake Check	Belts & Hoses

Note Repairs/Purchases

Mark C=Check or R=Replace

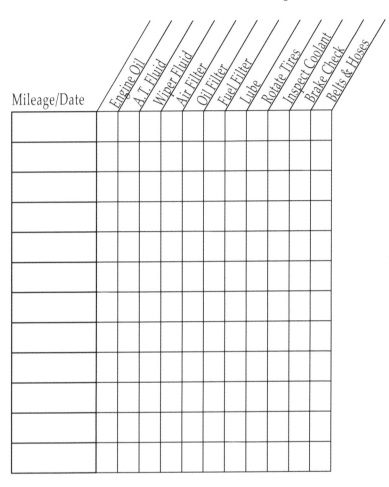

Mileage/Date	Engine Oil	A.T. Fluid	Wiper Fluid	Air Filter	Oil Filter	Fuel Filter	Lube	Rotate Tires	Inspect Coolant	Brake Check	Belts & Hoses

Note Repairs/Purchases

Mark C=Check or R=Replace

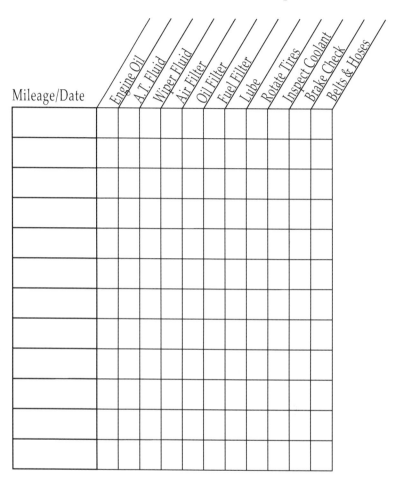

Mileage/Date	Engine Oil	A.T. Fluid	Wiper Fluid	Air Filter	Oil Filter	Fuel Filter	Lube	Rotate Tires	Inspect Coolant	Brake Check	Belts & Hoses

Note Repairs/Purchases

Mark C=Check or R=Replace

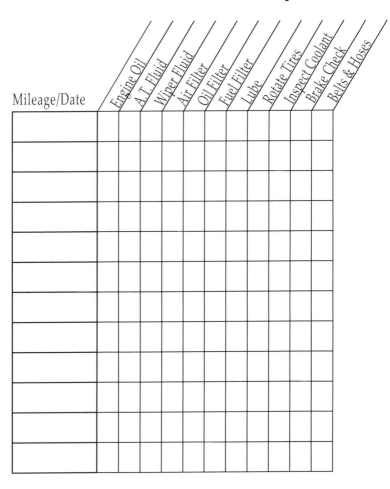

Mileage/Date | Engine Oil | A.T. Fluid | Wiper Fluid | Air Filter | Oil Filter | Fuel Filter | Lube | Rotate Tires | Inspect Coolant | Brake Check | Belts & Hoses

Note Repairs/Purchases

Mark C=Check or R=Replace

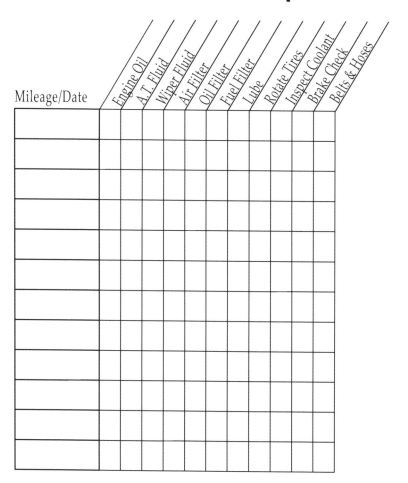

Mileage/Date	Engine Oil	A.T. Fluid	Wiper Fluid	Air Filter	Oil Filter	Fuel Filter	Lube	Rotate Tires	Inspect Coolant	Brake Check	Belts & Hoses

Note Repairs/Purchases

Mark C=Check or R=Replace

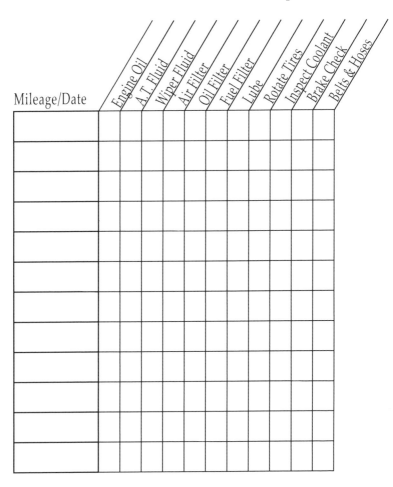

Mileage/Date	Engine Oil	A.T. Fluid	Wiper Fluid	Air Filter	Oil Filter	Fuel Filter	Lube	Rotate Tires	Inspect Coolant	Brake Check	Belts & Hoses

Note Repairs/Purchases

Mark C=Check or R=Replace

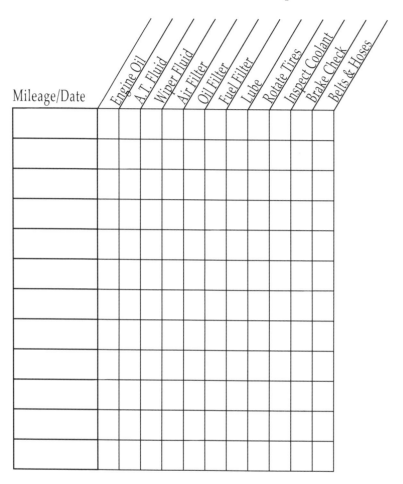

Mileage/Date	Engine Oil	A.T. Fluid	Wiper Fluid	Air Filter	Oil Filter	Fuel Filter	Lube	Rotate Tires	Inspect Coolant	Brake Check	Belts & Hoses

Note Repairs/Purchases

Mark C=Check or R=Replace

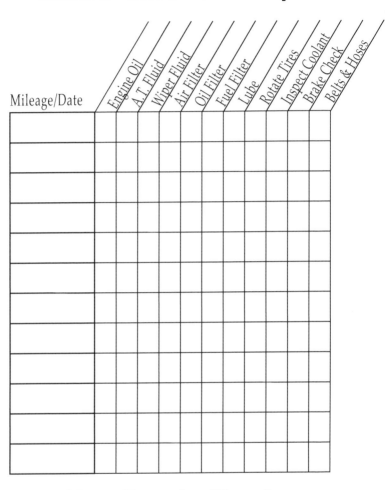

Mileage/Date	Engine Oil	A.T. Fluid	Wiper Fluid	Air Filter	Oil Filter	Fuel Filter	Lube	Rotate Tires	Inspect Coolant	Brake Check	Belts & Hoses

Note Repairs/Purchases

Mark C=Check or R=Replace

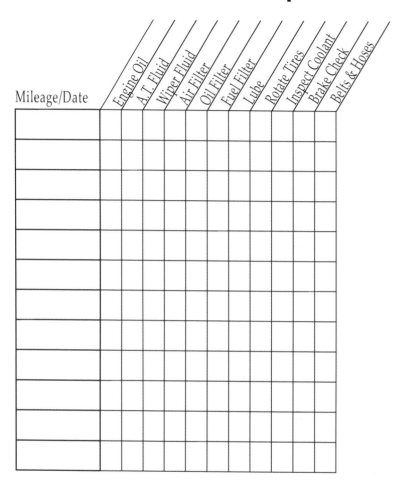

Mileage/Date	Engine Oil	A.T. Fluid	Wiper Fluid	Air Filter	Oil Filter	Fuel Filter	Lube	Rotate Tires	Inspect Coolant	Brake Check	Belts & Hoses

Note Repairs/Purchases

Mark C=Check or R=Replace

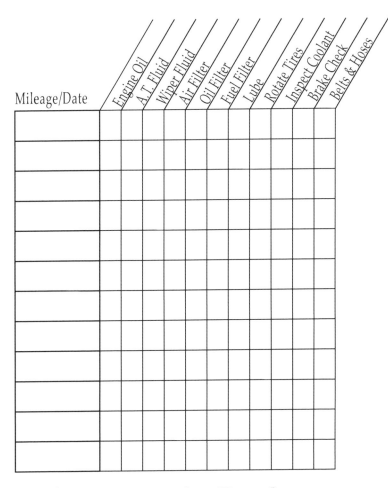

Mileage/Date	Engine Oil	A.T. Fluid	Wiper Fluid	Air Filter	Oil Filter	Fuel Filter	Lube	Rotate Tires	Inspect Coolant	Brake Check	Belts & Hoses

Note Repairs/Purchases

Mark C=Check or R=Replace

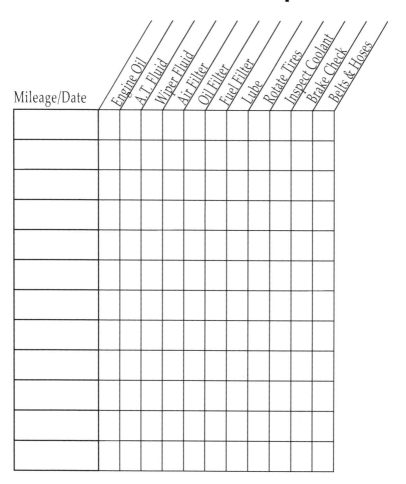

Mileage/Date	Engine Oil	A.T. Fluid	Wiper Fluid	Air Filter	Oil Filter	Fuel Filter	Lube	Rotate Tires	Inspect Coolant	Brake Check	Belts & Hoses

Note Repairs/Purchases

Mark C=Check or R=Replace

Mileage/Date	Engine Oil	A.T. Fluid	Wiper Fluid	Air Filter	Oil Filter	Fuel Filter	Lube	Rotate Tires	Inspect Coolant	Brake Check	Belts & Hoses

Note Repairs/Purchases

Mark C=Check or R=Replace

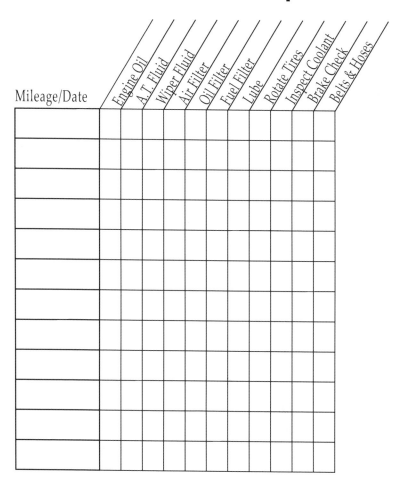

Mileage/Date	Engine Oil	A.T. Fluid	Wiper Fluid	Air Filter	Oil Filter	Fuel Filter	Lube	Rotate Tires	Inspect Coolant	Brake Check	Belts & Hoses

Note Repairs/Purchases

Mark C=Check or R=Replace

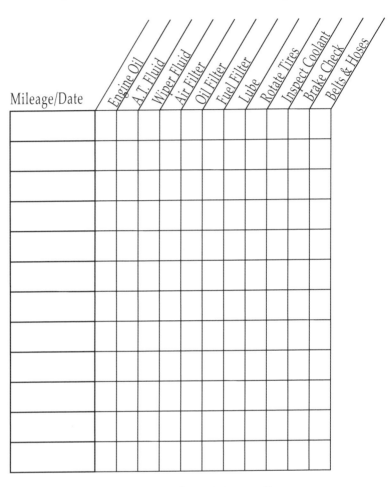

Mileage/Date	Engine Oil	A.T. Fluid	Wiper Fluid	Air Filter	Oil Filter	Fuel Filter	Lube	Rotate Tires	Inspect Coolant	Brake Check	Belts & Hoses

Note Repairs/Purchases

Mark C=Check or R=Replace

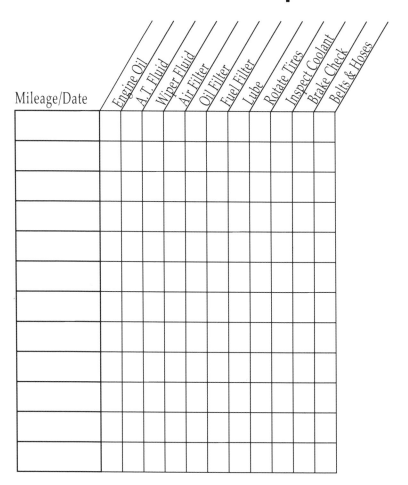

Mileage/Date	Engine Oil	A.T. Fluid	Wiper Fluid	Air Filter	Oil Filter	Fuel Filter	Lube	Rotate Tires	Inspect Coolant	Brake Check	Belts & Hoses

Note Repairs/Purchases

Mark C=Check or R=Replace

Mileage/Date	Engine Oil	A.T. Fluid	Wiper Fluid	Air Filter	Oil Filter	Fuel Filter	Lube	Rotate Tires	Inspect Coolant	Brake Check	Belts & Hoses

Note Repairs/Purchases

Mark C=Check or R=Replace

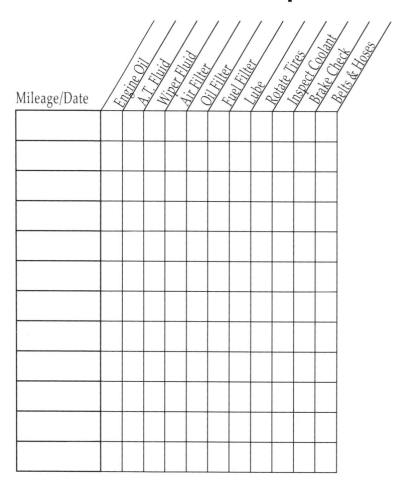

Mileage/Date	Engine Oil	A.T. Fluid	Wiper Fluid	Air Filter	Oil Filter	Fuel Filter	Lube	Rotate Tires	Inspect Coolant	Brake Check	Belts & Hoses

Note Repairs/Purchases

Mark C=Check or R=Replace

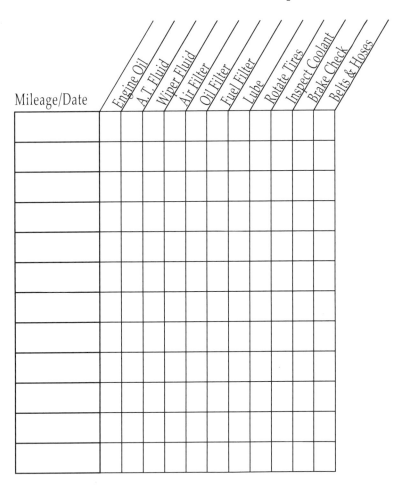

Mileage/Date	Engine Oil	A.T. Fluid	Wiper Fluid	Air Filter	Oil Filter	Fuel Filter	Lube	Rotate Tires	Inspect Coolant	Brake Check	Belts & Hoses

Note Repairs/Purchases

Mark C=Check or R=Replace

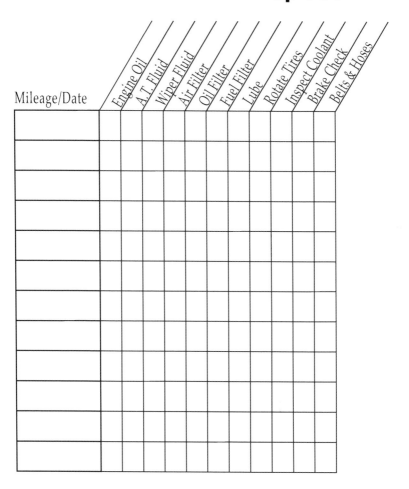

Mileage/Date	Engine Oil	A.T. Fluid	Wiper Fluid	Air Filter	Oil Filter	Fuel Filter	Lube	Rotate Tires	Inspect Coolant	Brake Check	Belts & Hoses

Note Repairs/Purchases

Mark C=Check or R=Replace

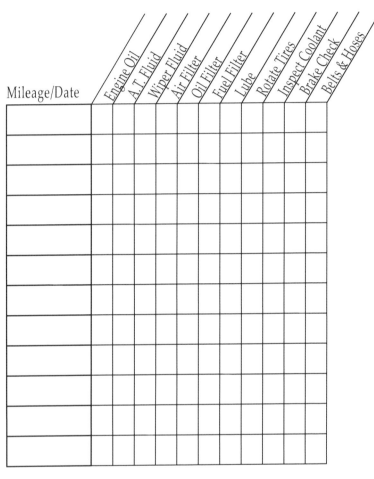

Mileage/Date	Engine Oil	A.T. Fluid	Wiper Fluid	Air Filter	Oil Filter	Fuel Filter	Lube	Rotate Tires	Inspect Coolant	Brake Check	Belts & Hoses

Note Repairs/Purchases

Mark C=Check or R=Replace

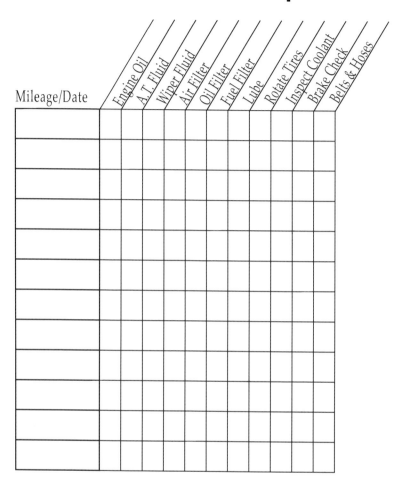

Mileage/Date	Engine Oil	A.T. Fluid	Wiper Fluid	Air Filter	Oil Filter	Fuel Filter	Lube	Rotate Tires	Inspect Coolant	Brake Check	Belts & Hoses

Note Repairs/Purchases

Mark C=Check or R=Replace

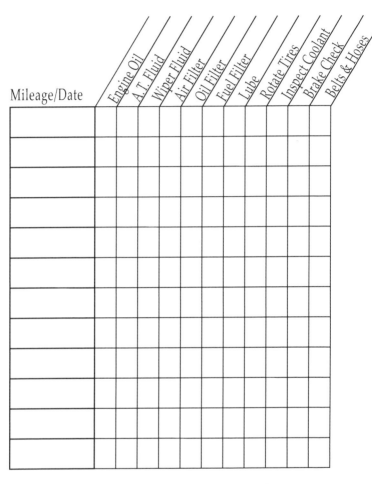

Mileage/Date	Engine Oil	A.T. Fluid	Wiper Fluid	Air Filter	Oil Filter	Fuel Filter	Lube	Rotate Tires	Inspect Coolant	Brake Check	Belts & Hoses

Note Repairs/Purchases

Mark C=Check or R=Replace

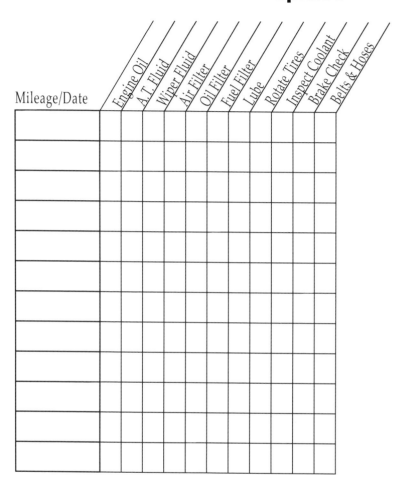

Mileage/Date	Engine Oil	A.T. Fluid	Wiper Fluid	Air Filter	Oil Filter	Fuel Filter	Lube	Rotate Tires	Inspect Coolant	Brake Check	Belts & Hoses

Note Repairs/Purchases

Mark C=Check or R=Replace

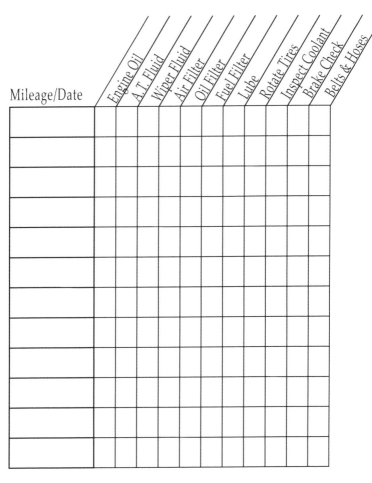

Mileage/Date	Engine Oil	A.T. Fluid	Wiper Fluid	Air Filter	Oil Filter	Fuel Filter	Lube	Rotate Tires	Inspect Coolant	Brake Check	Belts & Hoses

Note Repairs/Purchases

Mark C=Check or R=Replace

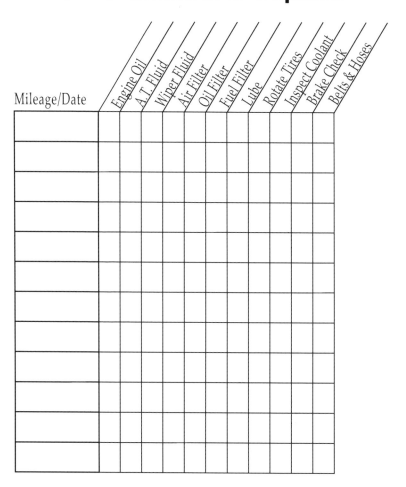

Mileage/Date	Engine Oil	A.T. Fluid	Wiper Fluid	Air Filter	Oil Filter	Fuel Filter	Lube	Rotate Tires	Inspect Coolant	Brake Check	Belts & Hoses

Note Repairs/Purchases

Mark C=Check or R=Replace

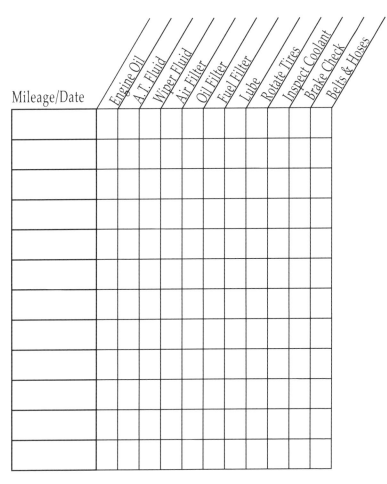

Mileage/Date	Engine Oil	A.T. Fluid	Wiper Fluid	Air Filter	Oil Filter	Fuel Filter	Lube	Rotate Tires	Inspect Coolant	Brake Check	Belts & Hoses

Note Repairs/Purchases

Mark C=Check or R=Replace

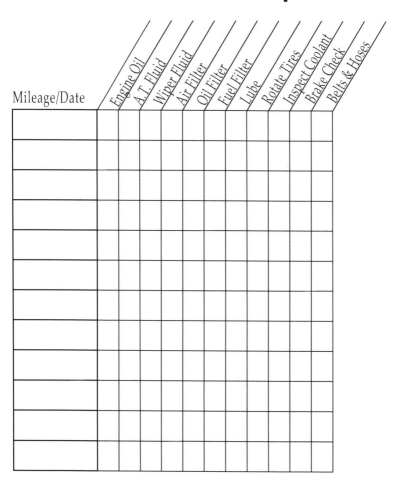

Mileage/Date	Engine Oil	A.T. Fluid	Wiper Fluid	Air Filter	Oil Filter	Fuel Filter	Lube	Rotate Tires	Inspect Coolant	Brake Check	Belts & Hoses

Note Repairs/Purchases

Mark C=Check or R=Replace

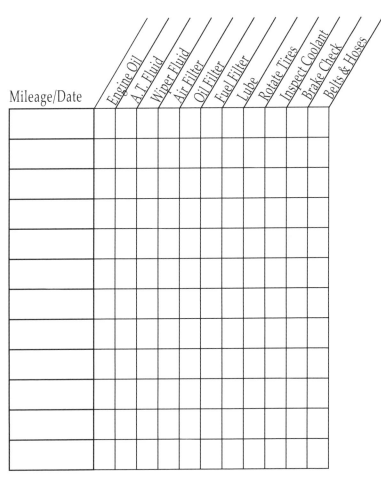

Mileage/Date	Engine Oil	A.T. Fluid	Wiper Fluid	Air Filter	Oil Filter	Fuel Filter	Lube	Rotate Tires	Inspect Coolant	Brake Check	Belts & Hoses

Note Repairs/Purchases

Mark C=Check or R=Replace

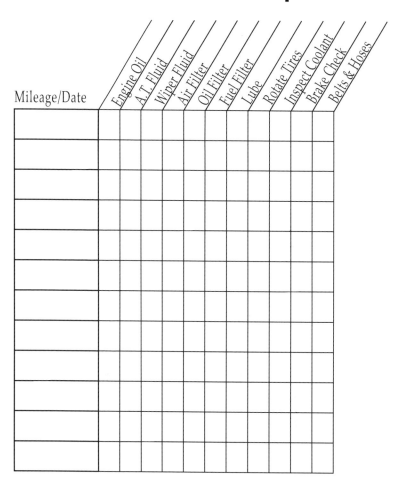

Mileage/Date	Engine Oil	A.T. Fluid	Wiper Fluid	Air Filter	Oil Filter	Fuel Filter	Lube	Rotate Tires	Inspect Coolant	Brake Check	Belts & Hoses

Note Repairs/Purchases

Mark C=Check or R=Replace

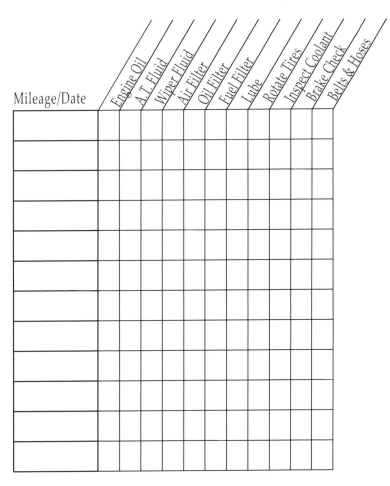

Mileage/Date	Engine Oil	A.T. Fluid	Wiper Fluid	Air Filter	Oil Filter	Fuel Filter	Lube	Rotate Tires	Inspect Coolant	Brake Check	Belts & Hoses

Note Repairs/Purchases

Mark C=Check or R=Replace

Mileage/Date	Engine Oil	A.T. Fluid	Wiper Fluid	Air Filter	Oil Filter	Fuel Filter	Lube	Rotate Tires	Inspect Coolant	Brake Check	Belts & Hoses

Note Repairs/Purchases

Mark C=Check or R=Replace

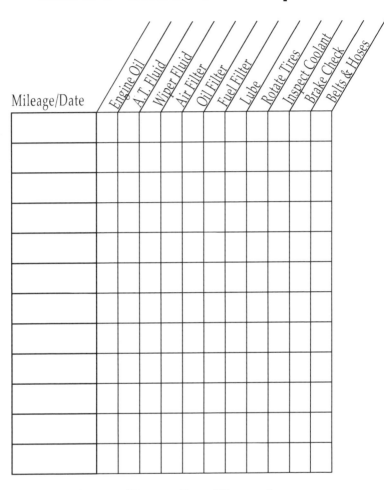

Mileage/Date	Engine Oil	A.T. Fluid	Wiper Fluid	Air Filter	Oil Filter	Fuel Filter	Lube	Rotate Tires	Inspect Coolant	Brake Check	Belts & Hoses

Note Repairs/Purchases

Mark C=Check or R=Replace

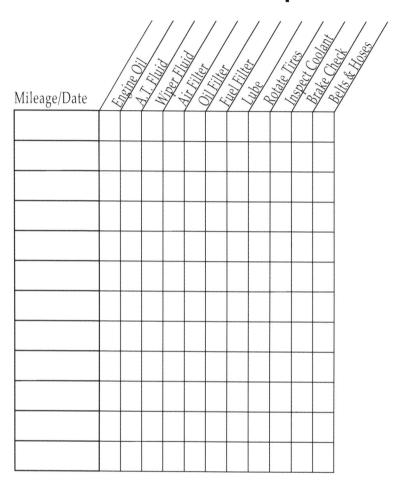

Mileage/Date	Engine Oil	A.T. Fluid	Wiper Fluid	Air Filter	Oil Filter	Fuel Filter	Lube	Rotate Tires	Inspect Coolant	Brake Check	Belts & Hoses

Note Repairs/Purchases

Mark C=Check or R=Replace

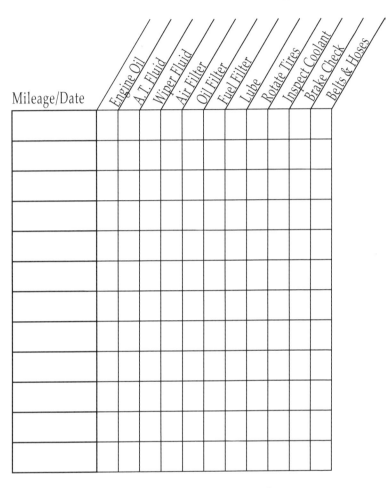

Mileage/Date	Engine Oil	A.T. Fluid	Wiper Fluid	Air Filter	Oil Filter	Fuel Filter	Lube	Rotate Tires	Inspect Coolant	Brake Check	Belts & Hoses

Note Repairs/Purchases

Mark C=Check or R=Replace

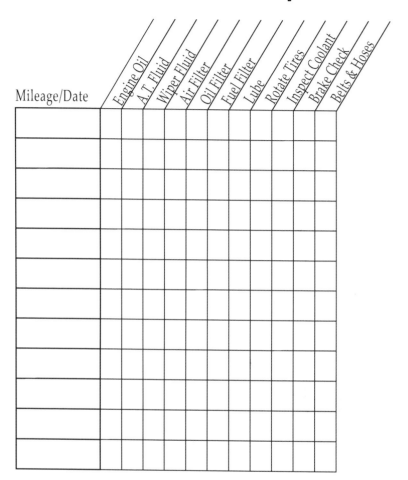

Mileage/Date	Engine Oil	A.T. Fluid	Wiper Fluid	Air Filter	Oil Filter	Fuel Filter	Lube	Rotate Tires	Inspect Coolant	Brake Check	Belts & Hoses

Note Repairs/Purchases

Mark C=Check or R=Replace

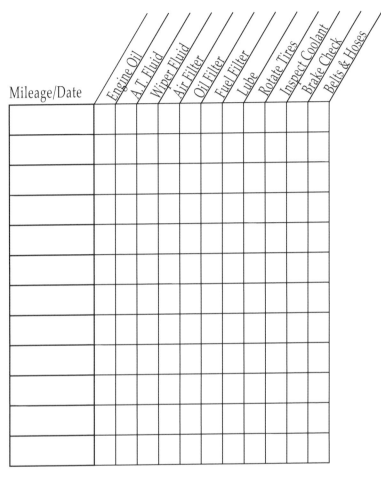

Mileage/Date	Engine Oil	A.T. Fluid	Wiper Fluid	Air Filter	Oil Filter	Fuel Filter	Lube	Rotate Tires	Inspect Coolant	Brake Check	Belts & Hoses

Note Repairs/Purchases

Mark C=Check or R=Replace

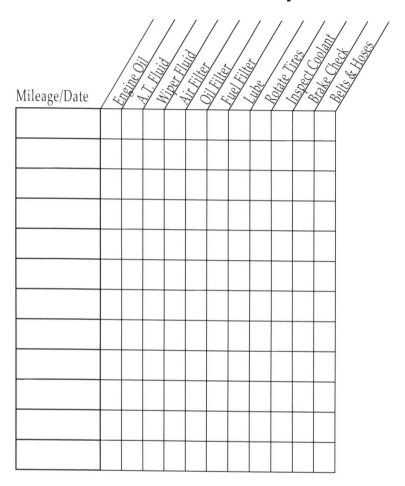

Mileage/Date	Engine Oil	A.T. Fluid	Wiper Fluid	Air Filter	Oil Filter	Fuel Filter	Lube	Rotate Tires	Inspect Coolant	Brake Check	Belts & Hoses

Note Repairs/Purchases

Mark C=Check or R=Replace

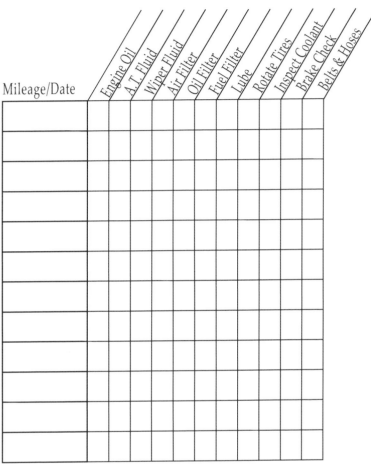

Mileage/Date	Engine Oil	A.T. Fluid	Wiper Fluid	Air Filter	Oil Filter	Fuel Filter	Lube	Rotate Tires	Inspect Coolant	Brake Check	Belts & Hoses

Note Repairs/Purchases

Mark C=Check or R=Replace

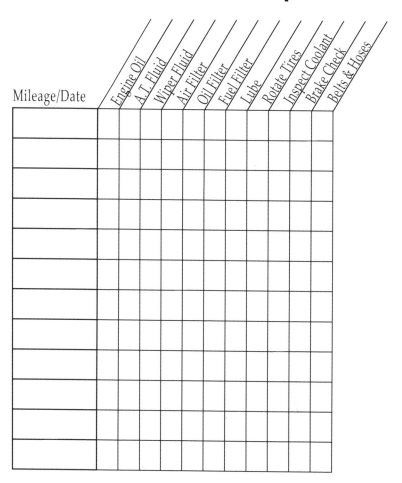

Mileage/Date	Engine Oil	A.T. Fluid	Wiper Fluid	Air Filter	Oil Filter	Fuel Filter	Lube	Rotate Tires	Inspect Coolant	Brake Check	Belts & Hoses

Note Repairs/Purchases

Mark C=Check or R=Replace

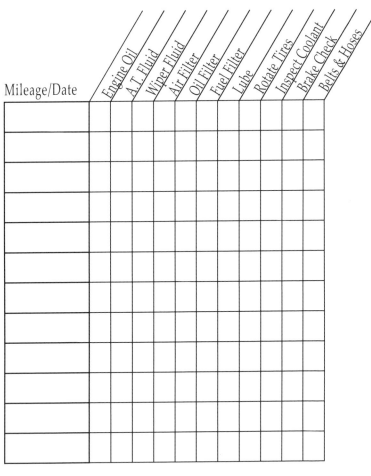

Mileage/Date	Engine Oil	A.T. Fluid	Wiper Fluid	Air Filter	Oil Filter	Fuel Filter	Lube	Rotate Tires	Inspect Coolant	Brake Check	Belts & Hoses

Note Repairs/Purchases

Mark C=Check or R=Replace

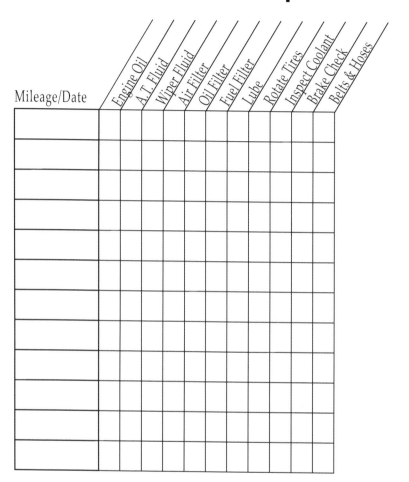

Mileage/Date	Engine Oil	A.T. Fluid	Wiper Fluid	Air Filter	Oil Filter	Fuel Filter	Lube	Rotate Tires	Inspect Coolant	Brake Check	Belts & Hoses

Note Repairs/Purchases

Mark C=Check or R=Replace

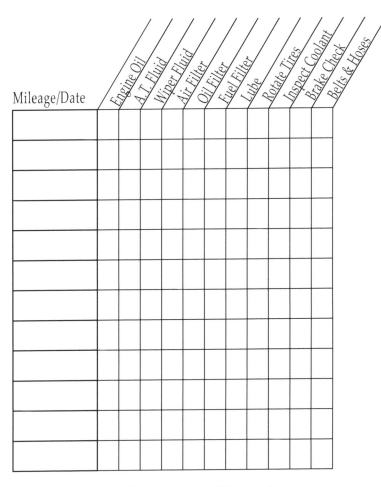

Mileage/Date	Engine Oil	A.T. Fluid	Wiper Fluid	Air Filter	Oil Filter	Fuel Filter	Lube	Rotate Tires	Inspect Coolant	Brake Check	Belts & Hoses

Note Repairs/Purchases

Mark C=Check or R=Replace

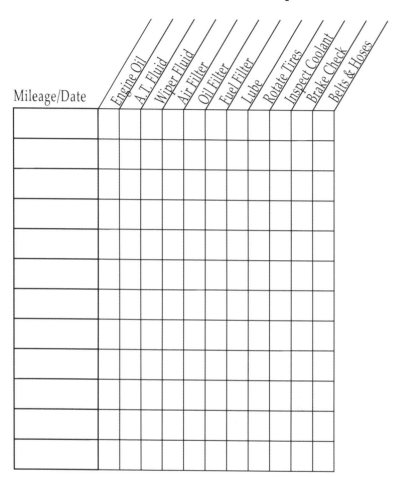

Mileage/Date	Engine Oil	A.T. Fluid	Wiper Fluid	Air Filter	Oil Filter	Fuel Filter	Lube	Rotate Tires	Inspect Coolant	Brake Check	Belts & Hoses

Note Repairs/Purchases

Mark C=Check or R=Replace

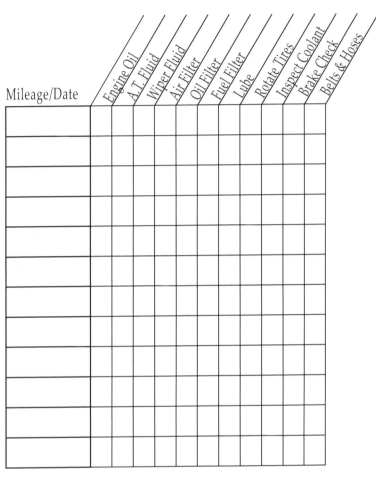

Mileage/Date	Engine Oil	A.T. Fluid	Wiper Fluid	Air Filter	Oil Filter	Fuel Filter	Lube	Rotate Tires	Inspect Coolant	Brake Check	Belts & Hoses

Note Repairs/Purchases

Mark C=Check or R=Replace

Mileage/Date	Engine Oil	A.T. Fluid	Wiper Fluid	Air Filter	Oil Filter	Fuel Filter	Lube	Rotate Tires	Inspect Coolant	Brake Check	Belts & Hoses

Note Repairs/Purchases

Mark C=Check or R=Replace

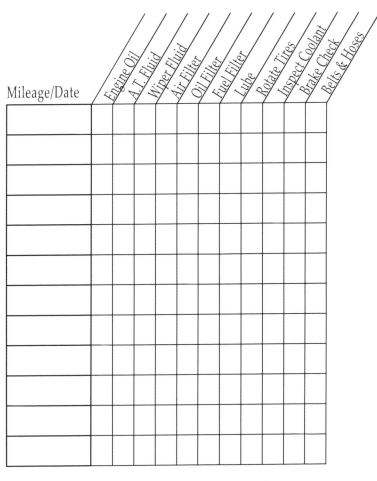

Mileage/Date	Engine Oil	A.T. Fluid	Wiper Fluid	Air Filter	Oil Filter	Fuel Filter	Lube	Rotate Tires	Inspect Coolant	Brake Check	Belts & Hoses

Note Repairs/Purchases

Mark C=Check or R=Replace

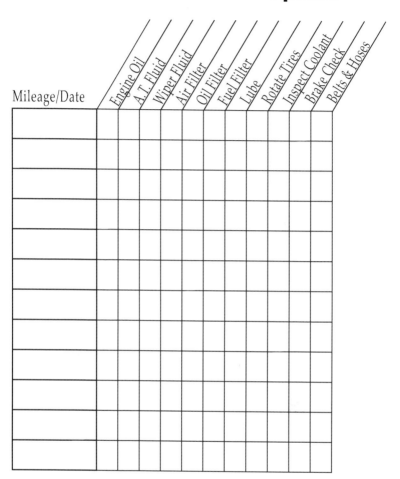

Mileage/Date	Engine Oil	A.T. Fluid	Wiper Fluid	Air Filter	Oil Filter	Fuel Filter	Lube	Rotate Tires	Inspect Coolant	Brake Check	Belts & Hoses

Note Repairs/Purchases

Mark C=Check or R=Replace

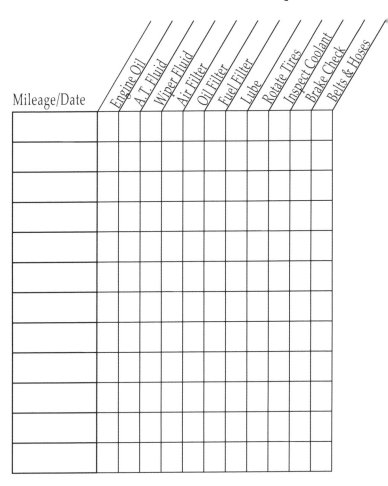

Mileage/Date	Engine Oil	A.T. Fluid	Wiper Fluid	Air Filter	Oil Filter	Fuel Filter	Lube	Rotate Tires	Inspect Coolant	Brake Check	Belts & Hoses

Note Repairs/Purchases

Mark C=Check or R=Replace

Mileage/Date	Engine Oil	A.T. Fluid	Wiper Fluid	Air Filter	Oil Filter	Fuel Filter	Lube	Rotate Tires	Inspect Coolant	Brake Check	Belts & Hoses

Note Repairs/Purchases

Mark C=Check or R=Replace

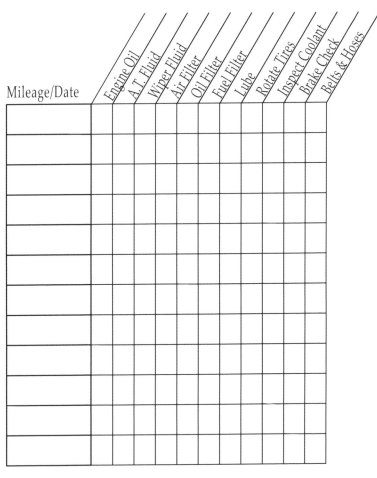

Mileage/Date	Engine Oil	A.T. Fluid	Wiper Fluid	Air Filter	Oil Filter	Fuel Filter	Lube	Rotate Tires	Inspect Coolant	Brake Check	Belts & Hoses

Note Repairs/Purchases

Mark C=Check or R=Replace

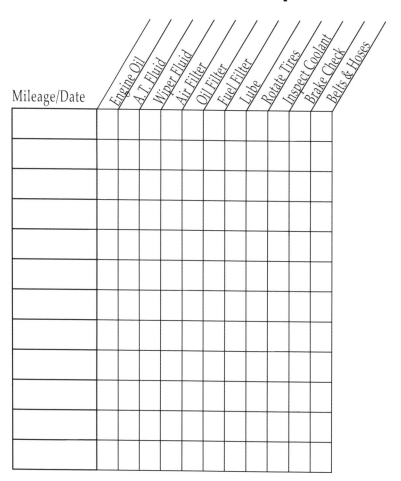

Mileage/Date	Engine Oil	A.T. Fluid	Wiper Fluid	Air Filter	Oil Filter	Fuel Filter	Lube	Rotate Tires	Inspect Coolant	Brake Check	Belts & Hoses

Note Repairs/Purchases

Mark C=Check or R=Replace

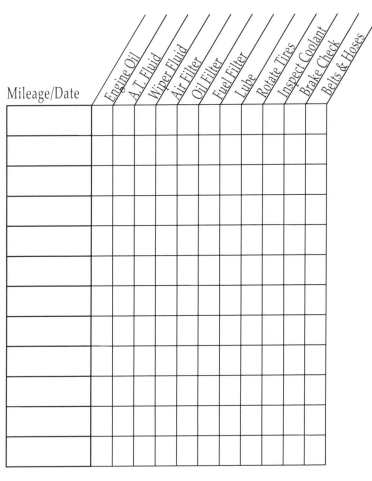

Mileage/Date	Engine Oil	A.T. Fluid	Wiper Fluid	Air Filter	Oil Filter	Fuel Filter	Lube	Rotate Tires	Inspect Coolant	Brake Check	Belts & Hoses

Note Repairs/Purchases

Mark C=Check or R=Replace

Mileage/Date	Engine Oil	A.T. Fluid	Wiper Fluid	Air Filter	Oil Filter	Fuel Filter	Lube	Rotate Tires	Inspect Coolant	Brake Check	Belts & Hoses

Note Repairs/Purchases

Mark C=Check or R=Replace

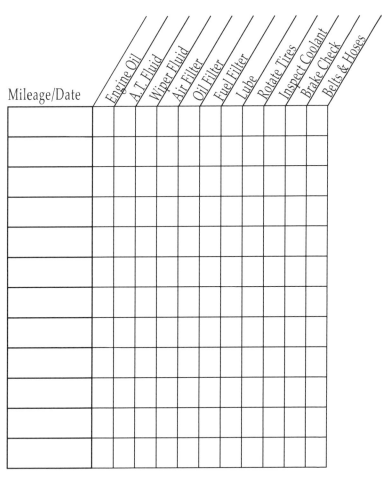

Mileage/Date	Engine Oil	A.T. Fluid	Wiper Fluid	Air Filter	Oil Filter	Fuel Filter	Lube	Rotate Tires	Inspect Coolant	Brake Check	Belts & Hoses

Note Repairs/Purchases

Mark C=Check or R=Replace

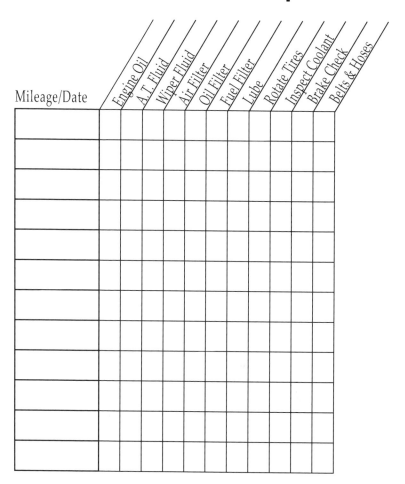

Mileage/Date	Engine Oil	A.T. Fluid	Wiper Fluid	Air Filter	Oil Filter	Fuel Filter	Lube	Rotate Tires	Inspect Coolant	Brake Check	Belts & Hoses

Note Repairs/Purchases

Mark C=Check or R=Replace

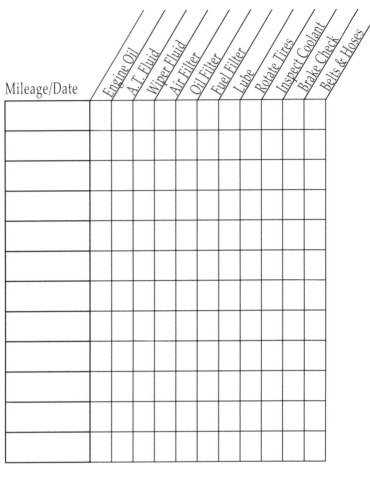

Mileage/Date	Engine Oil	A.T. Fluid	Wiper Fluid	Air Filter	Oil Filter	Fuel Filter	Lube	Rotate Tires	Inspect Coolant	Brake Check	Belts & Hoses

Note Repairs/Purchases

Mark C=Check or R=Replace

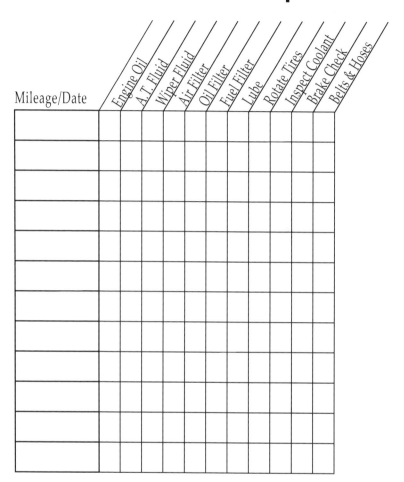

Mileage/Date	Engine Oil	A.T. Fluid	Wiper Fluid	Air Filter	Oil Filter	Fuel Filter	Lube	Rotate Tires	Inspect Coolant	Brake Check	Belts & Hoses

Note Repairs/Purchases

Mark C=Check or R=Replace

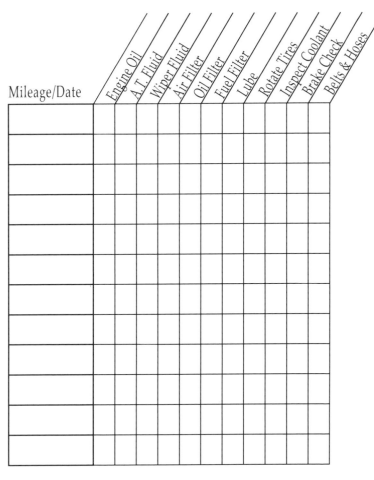

Mileage/Date	Engine Oil	A.T. Fluid	Wiper Fluid	Air Filter	Oil Filter	Fuel Filter	Lube	Rotate Tires	Inspect Coolant	Brake Check	Belts & Hoses

Note Repairs/Purchases

Mark C=Check or R=Replace

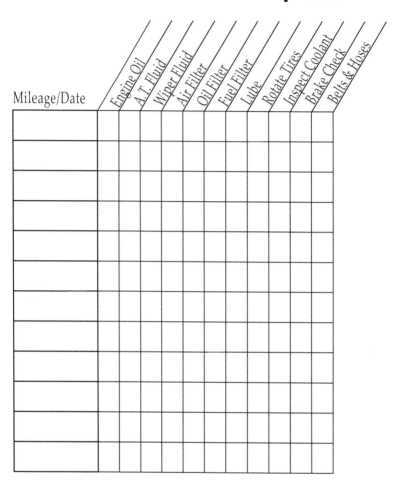

Mileage/Date	Engine Oil	A.T. Fluid	Wiper Fluid	Air Filter	Oil Filter	Fuel Filter	Lube	Rotate Tires	Inspect Coolant	Brake Check	Belts & Hoses

Note Repairs/Purchases

Mark C=Check or R=Replace

Mileage/Date	Engine Oil	A.T. Fluid	Wiper Fluid	Air Filter	Oil Filter	Fuel Filter	Lube	Rotate Tires	Inspect Coolant	Brake Check	Belts & Hoses

Note Repairs/Purchases

Mark C=Check or R=Replace

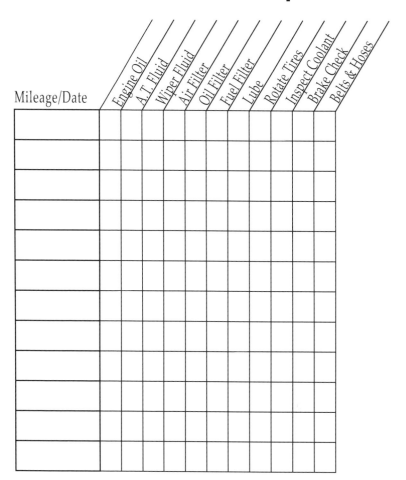

Mileage/Date	Engine Oil	A.T. Fluid	Wiper Fluid	Air Filter	Oil Filter	Fuel Filter	Lube	Rotate Tires	Inspect Coolant	Brake Check	Belts & Hoses

Note Repairs/Purchases

Mark C=Check or R=Replace

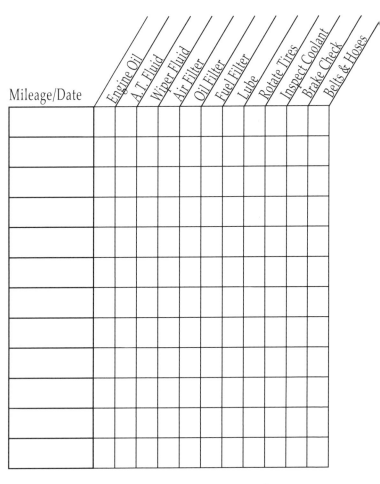

Mileage/Date	Engine Oil	A.T. Fluid	Wiper Fluid	Air Filter	Oil Filter	Fuel Filter	Lube	Rotate Tires	Inspect Coolant	Brake Check	Belts & Hoses

Note Repairs/Purchases

Mark C=Check or R=Replace

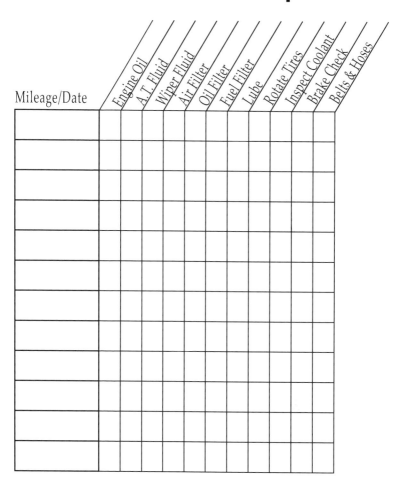

Mileage/Date	Engine Oil	A.T. Fluid	Wiper Fluid	Air Filter	Oil Filter	Fuel Filter	Lube	Rotate Tires	Inspect Coolant	Brake Check	Belts & Hoses

Note Repairs/Purchases

Mark C=Check or R=Replace

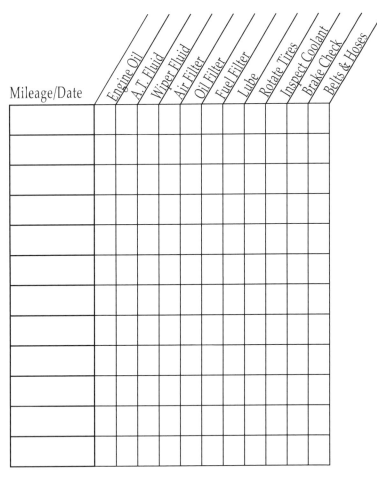

Mileage/Date	Engine Oil	A.T. Fluid	Wiper Fluid	Air Filter	Oil Filter	Fuel Filter	Lube	Rotate Tires	Inspect Coolant	Brake Check	Belts & Hoses

Note Repairs/Purchases

Mark C=Check or R=Replace

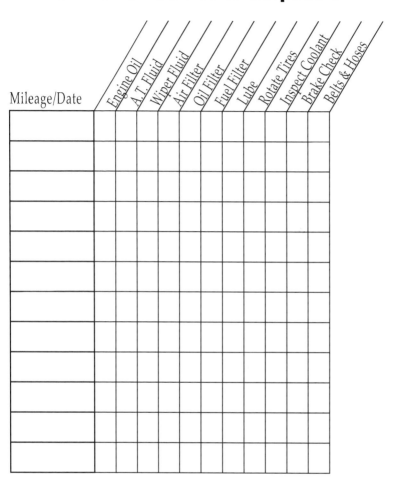

Mileage/Date	Engine Oil	A.T. Fluid	Wiper Fluid	Air Filter	Oil Filter	Fuel Filter	Lube	Rotate Tires	Inspect Coolant	Brake Check	Belts & Hoses

Note Repairs/Purchases

Mark C=Check or R=Replace

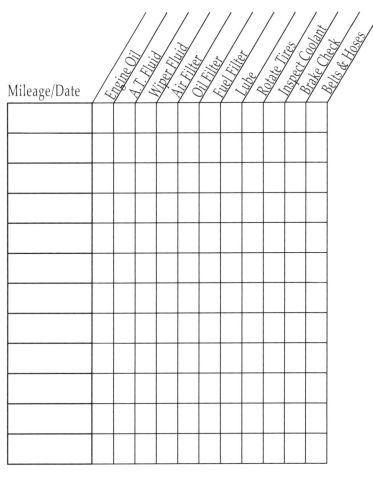

Mileage/Date	Engine Oil	A.T. Fluid	Wiper Fluid	Air Filter	Oil Filter	Fuel Filter	Lube	Rotate Tires	Inspect Coolant	Brake Check	Belts & Hoses

Note Repairs/Purchases

Mark C=Check or R=Replace

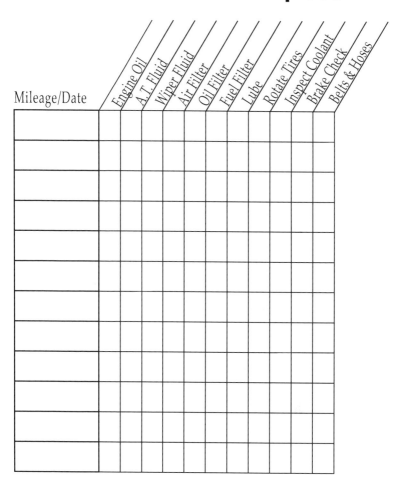

Mileage/Date	Engine Oil	A.T. Fluid	Wiper Fluid	Air Filter	Oil Filter	Fuel Filter	Lube	Rotate Tires	Inspect Coolant	Brake Check	Belts & Hoses

Note Repairs/Purchases

Mark C=Check or R=Replace

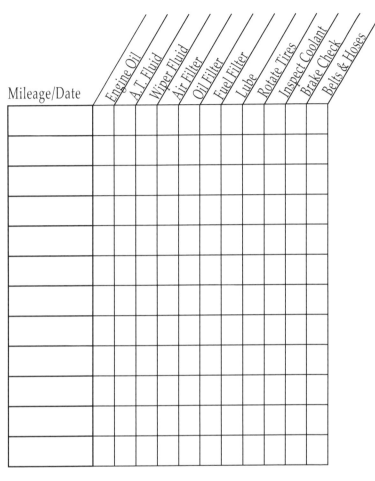

Mileage/Date	Engine Oil	A.T. Fluid	Wiper Fluid	Air Filter	Oil Filter	Fuel Filter	Lube	Rotate Tires	Inspect Coolant	Brake Check	Belts & Hoses

Note Repairs/Purchases

Mark C=Check or R=Replace

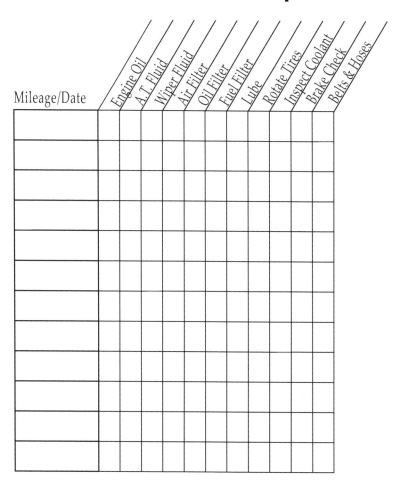

Mileage/Date	Engine Oil	A.T. Fluid	Wiper Fluid	Air Filter	Oil Filter	Fuel Filter	Lube	Rotate Tires	Inspect Coolant	Brake Check	Belts & Hoses

Note Repairs/Purchases

Mark C=Check or R=Replace

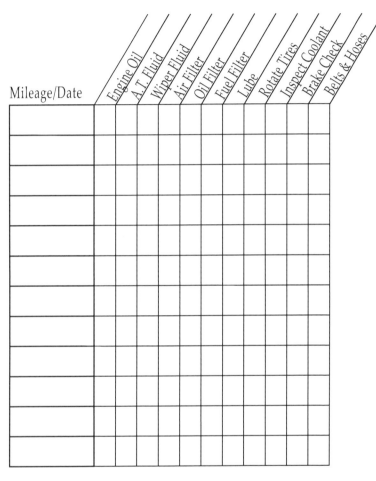

Mileage/Date	Engine Oil	A.T. Fluid	Wiper Fluid	Air Filter	Oil Filter	Fuel Filter	Lube	Rotate Tires	Inspect Coolant	Brake Check	Belts & Hoses

Note Repairs/Purchases

Mark C=Check or R=Replace

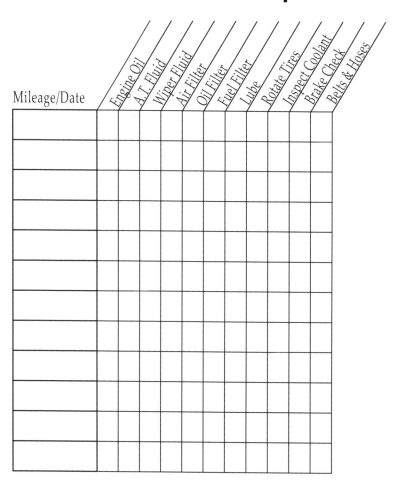

Mileage/Date	Engine Oil	A.T. Fluid	Wiper Fluid	Air Filter	Oil Filter	Fuel Filter	Lube	Rotate Tires	Inspect Coolant	Brake Check	Belts & Hoses

Note Repairs/Purchases

Mark C=Check or R=Replace

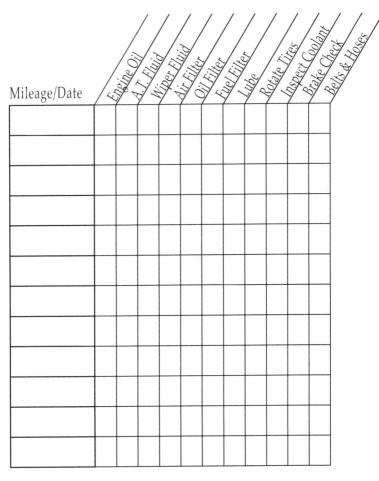

Mileage/Date	Engine Oil	A.T. Fluid	Wiper Fluid	Air Filter	Oil Filter	Fuel Filter	Lube	Rotate Tires	Inspect Coolant	Brake Check	Belts & Hoses

Note Repairs/Purchases

Mark C=Check or R=Replace

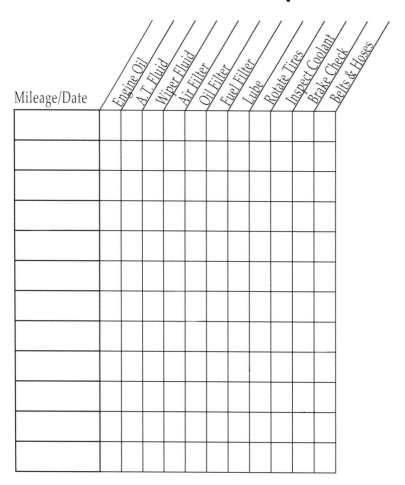

Mileage/Date	Engine Oil	A.T. Fluid	Wiper Fluid	Air Filter	Oil Filter	Fuel Filter	Lube	Rotate Tires	Inspect Coolant	Brake Check	Belts & Hoses

Note Repairs/Purchases

Mark C=Check or R=Replace

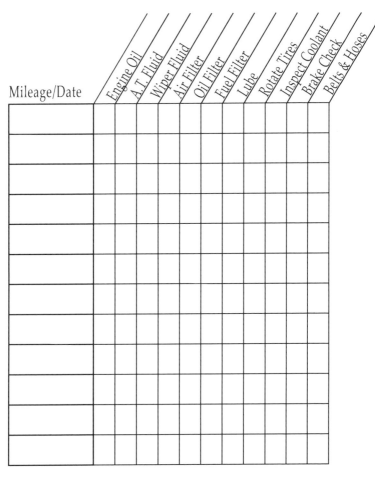

Mileage/Date	Engine Oil	A.T. Fluid	Wiper Fluid	Air Filter	Oil Filter	Fuel Filter	Lube	Rotate Tires	Inspect Coolant	Brake Check	Belts & Hoses

Note Repairs/Purchases

Mark C=Check or R=Replace

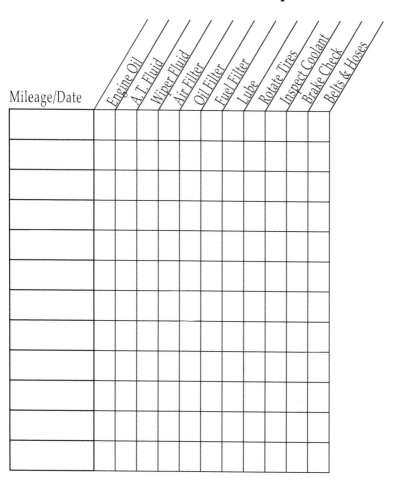

Mileage/Date	Engine Oil	A.T. Fluid	Wiper Fluid	Air Filter	Oil Filter	Fuel Filter	Lube	Rotate Tires	Inspect Coolant	Brake Check	Belts & Hoses

Note Repairs/Purchases

Mark C=Check or R=Replace

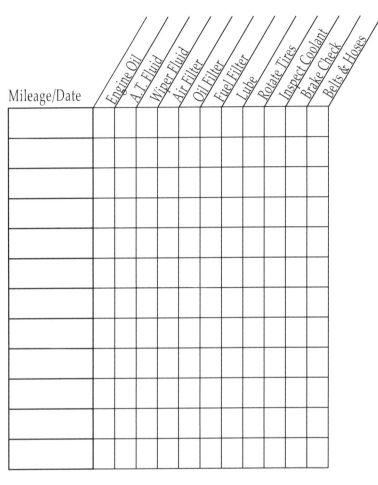

Mileage/Date	Engine Oil	A.T. Fluid	Wiper Fluid	Air Filter	Oil Filter	Fuel Filter	Lube	Rotate Tires	Inspect Coolant	Brake Check	Belts & Hoses

Note Repairs/Purchases

Mark C=Check or R=Replace

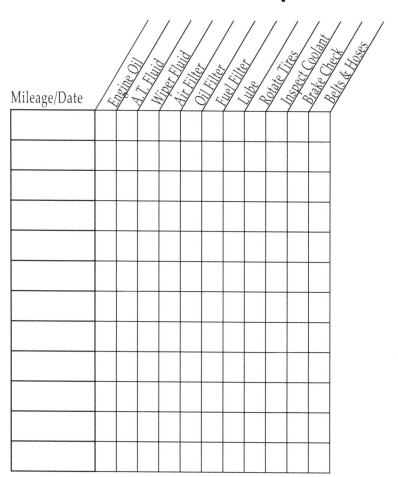

Mileage/Date	Engine Oil	A.T. Fluid	Wiper Fluid	Air Filter	Oil Filter	Fuel Filter	Lube	Rotate Tires	Inspect Coolant	Brake Check	Belts & Hoses

Note Repairs/Purchases

Mark C=Check or R=Replace

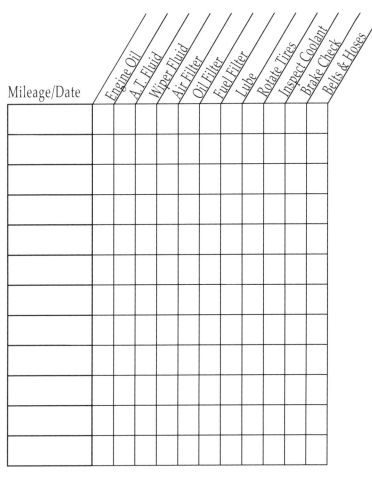

Mileage/Date	Engine Oil	A.T. Fluid	Wiper Fluid	Air Filter	Oil Filter	Fuel Filter	Lube	Rotate Tires	Inspect Coolant	Brake Check	Belts & Hoses

Note Repairs/Purchases

Mark C=Check or R=Replace

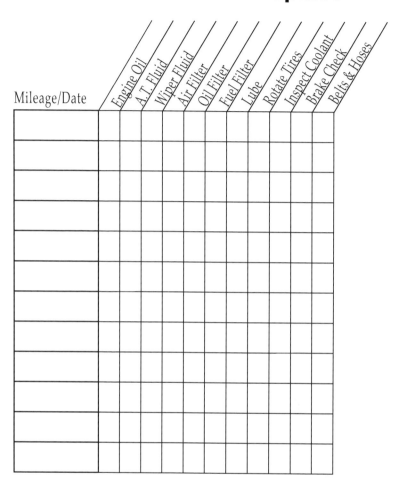

Mileage/Date	Engine Oil	A.T. Fluid	Wiper Fluid	Air Filter	Oil Filter	Fuel Filter	Lube	Rotate Tires	Inspect Coolant	Brake Check	Belts & Hoses

Note Repairs/Purchases

Mark C=Check or R=Replace

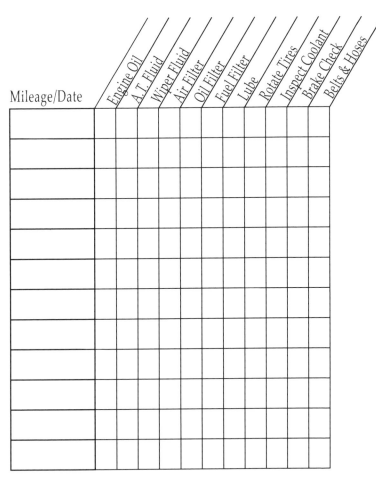

Mileage/Date	Engine Oil	A.T. Fluid	Wiper Fluid	Air Filter	Oil Filter	Fuel Filter	Lube	Rotate Tires	Inspect Coolant	Brake Check	Belts & Hoses

Note Repairs/Purchases

Mark C=Check or R=Replace

Mileage/Date	Engine Oil	A.T. Fluid	Wiper Fluid	Air Filter	Oil Filter	Fuel Filter	Lube	Rotate Tires	Inspect Coolant	Brake Check	Belts & Hoses

Note Repairs/Purchases

Mark C=Check or R=Replace

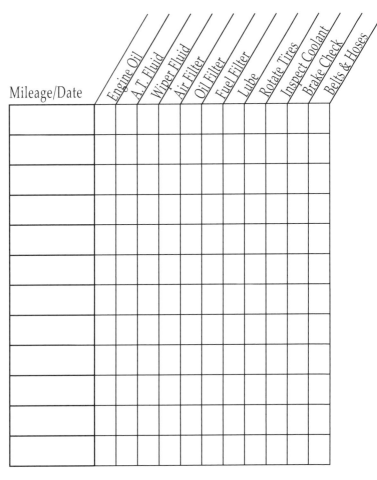

Mileage/Date	Engine Oil	A.T. Fluid	Wiper Fluid	Air Filter	Oil Filter	Fuel Filter	Lube	Rotate Tires	Inspect Coolant	Brake Check	Belts & Hoses

Note Repairs/Purchases

Mark C=Check or R=Replace

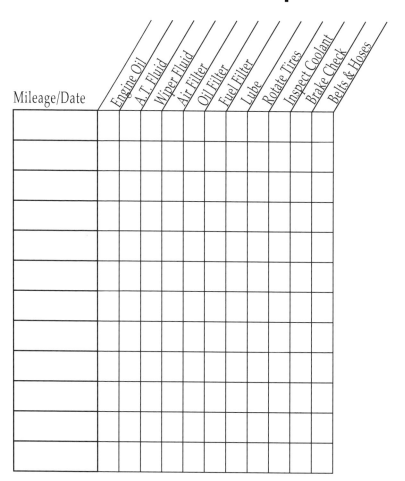

Mileage/Date	Engine Oil	A.T. Fluid	Wiper Fluid	Air Filter	Oil Filter	Fuel Filter	Lube	Rotate Tires	Inspect Coolant	Brake Check	Belts & Hoses

Note Repairs/Purchases

Mark C=Check or R=Replace

Mileage/Date	Engine Oil	A.T. Fluid	Wiper Fluid	Air Filter	Oil Filter	Fuel Filter	Lube	Rotate Tires	Inspect Coolant	Brake Check	Belts & Hoses

Note Repairs/Purchases

Mark C=Check or R=Replace

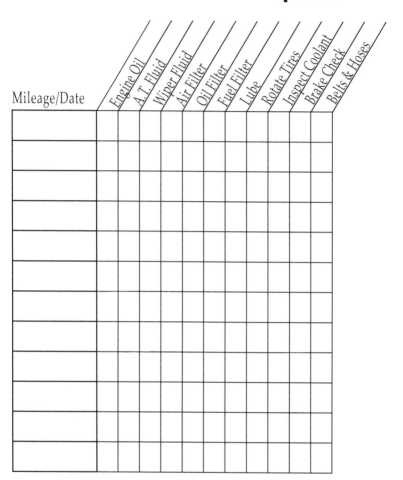

Mileage/Date	Engine Oil	A.T. Fluid	Wiper Fluid	Air Filter	Oil Filter	Fuel Filter	Lube	Rotate Tires	Inspect Coolant	Brake Check	Belts & Hoses

Note Repairs/Purchases

Mark C=Check or R=Replace

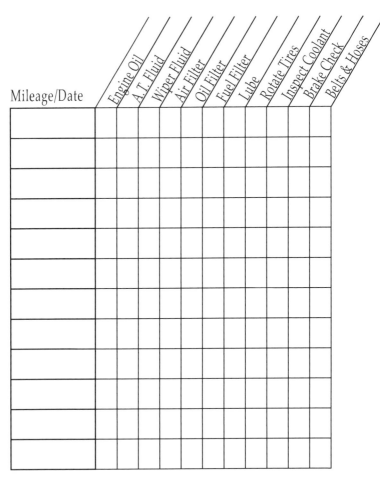

Mileage/Date | Engine Oil | A.T. Fluid | Wiper Fluid | Air Filter | Oil Filter | Fuel Filter | Lube | Rotate Tires | Inspect Coolant | Brake Check | Belts & Hoses

Note Repairs/Purchases

Mark C=Check or R=Replace

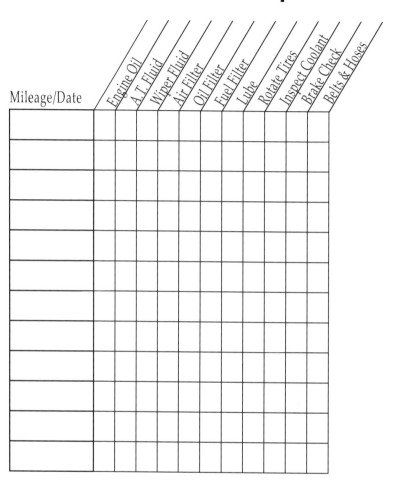

Mileage/Date	Engine Oil	A.T. Fluid	Wiper Fluid	Air Filter	Oil Filter	Fuel Filter	Lube	Rotate Tires	Inspect Coolant	Brake Check	Belts & Hoses

Note Repairs/Purchases

Mark C=Check or R=Replace

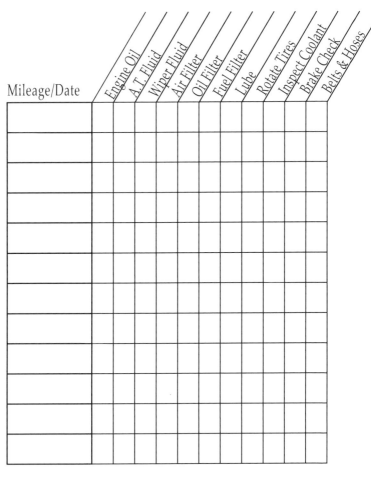

Mileage/Date	Engine Oil	A.T. Fluid	Wiper Fluid	Air Filter	Oil Filter	Fuel Filter	Lube	Rotate Tires	Inspect Coolant	Brake Check	Belts & Hoses

Note Repairs/Purchases

Mark C=Check or R=Replace

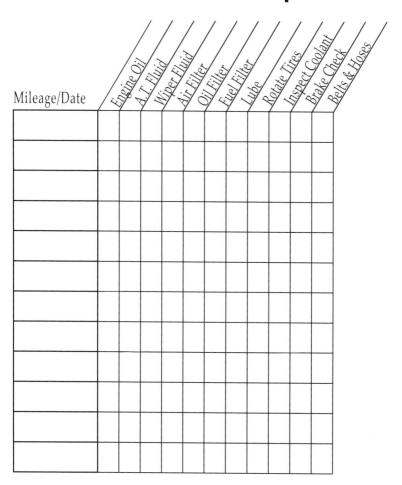

Mileage/Date	Engine Oil	A.T. Fluid	Wiper Fluid	Air Filter	Oil Filter	Fuel Filter	Lube	Rotate Tires	Inspect Coolant	Brake Check	Belts & Hoses

Note Repairs/Purchases

Mark C=Check or R=Replace

Mileage/Date	Engine Oil	A.T. Fluid	Wiper Fluid	Air Filter	Oil Filter	Fuel Filter	Lube	Rotate Tires	Inspect Coolant	Brake Check	Belts & Hoses

Note Repairs/Purchases

Mark C=Check or R=Replace

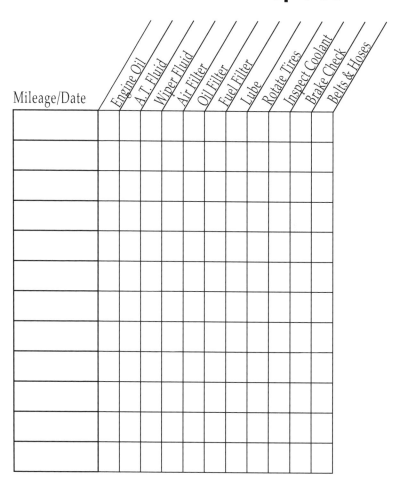

Mileage/Date	Engine Oil	A.T. Fluid	Wiper Fluid	Air Filter	Oil Filter	Fuel Filter	Lube	Rotate Tires	Inspect Coolant	Brake Check	Belts & Hoses

Note Repairs/Purchases

Mark C=Check or R=Replace

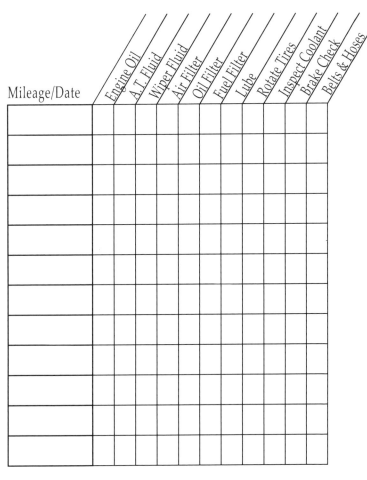

Mileage/Date	Engine Oil	A.T. Fluid	Wiper Fluid	Air Filter	Oil Filter	Fuel Filter	Lube	Rotate Tires	Inspect Coolant	Brake Check	Belts & Hoses

Note Repairs/Purchases

Mark C=Check or R=Replace

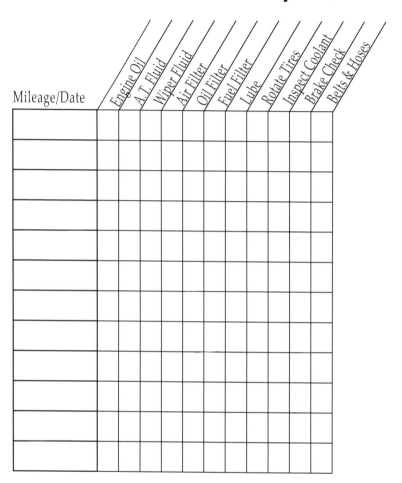

Mileage/Date	Engine Oil	A.T. Fluid	Wiper Fluid	Air Filter	Oil Filter	Fuel Filter	Lube	Rotate Tires	Inspect Coolant	Brake Check	Belts & Hoses

Note Repairs/Purchases

Mark C=Check or R=Replace

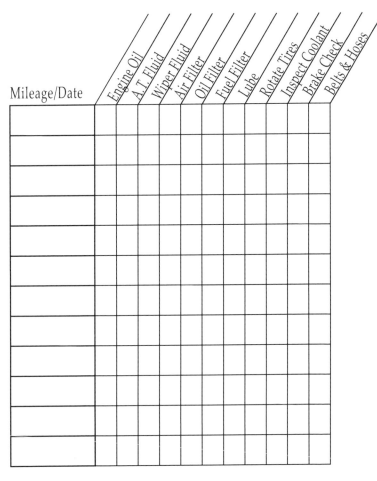

Mileage/Date	Engine Oil	A.T. Fluid	Wiper Fluid	Air Filter	Oil Filter	Fuel Filter	Lube	Rotate Tires	Inspect Coolant	Brake Check	Belts & Hoses

Note Repairs/Purchases

Mark C=Check or R=Replace

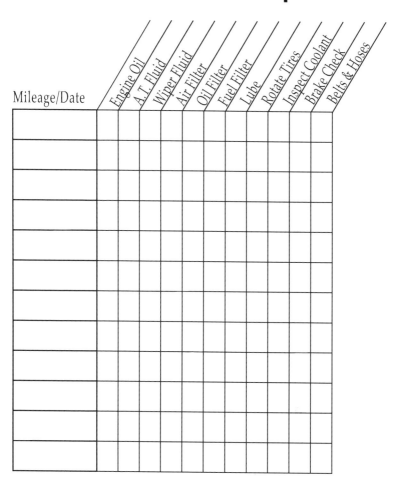

Mileage/Date	Engine Oil	A.T. Fluid	Wiper Fluid	Air Filter	Oil Filter	Fuel Filter	Lube	Rotate Tires	Inspect Coolant	Brake Check	Belts & Hoses

Note Repairs/Purchases

Mark C=Check or R=Replace

Mileage/Date	Engine Oil	A.T. Fluid	Wiper Fluid	Air Filter	Oil Filter	Fuel Filter	Lube	Rotate Tires	Inspect Coolant	Brake Check	Belts & Hoses

Note Repairs/Purchases

Mark C=Check or R=Replace

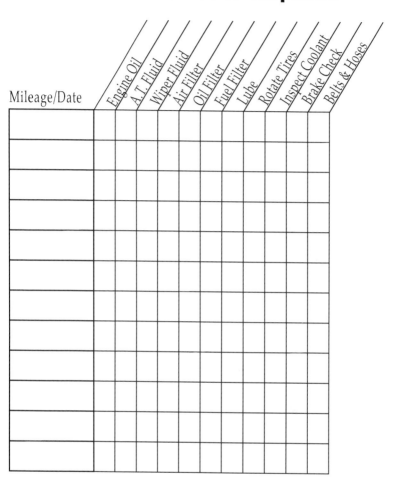

Mileage/Date	Engine Oil	A.T. Fluid	Wiper Fluid	Air Filter	Oil Filter	Fuel Filter	Lube	Rotate Tires	Inspect Coolant	Brake Check	Belts & Hoses

Note Repairs/Purchases

Mark C=Check or R=Replace

Mileage/Date	Engine Oil	A.T. Fluid	Wiper Fluid	Air Filter	Oil Filter	Fuel Filter	Lube	Rotate Tires	Inspect Coolant	Brake Check	Belts & Hoses

Note Repairs/Purchases

Mark C=Check or R=Replace

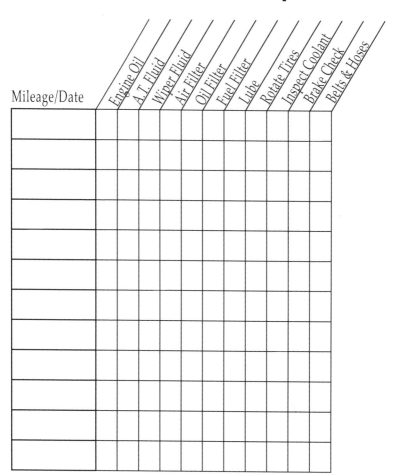

Mileage/Date	Engine Oil	A.T. Fluid	Wiper Fluid	Air Filter	Oil Filter	Fuel Filter	Lube	Rotate Tires	Inspect Coolant	Brake Check	Belts & Hoses

Note Repairs/Purchases

Mark C=Check or R=Replace

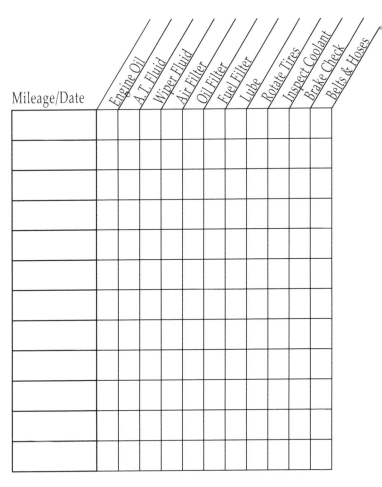

Mileage/Date	Engine Oil	A.T. Fluid	Wiper Fluid	Air Filter	Oil Filter	Fuel Filter	Lube	Rotate Tires	Inspect Coolant	Brake Check	Belts & Hoses

Note Repairs/Purchases

Mark C=Check or R=Replace

Mileage/Date	Engine Oil	A.T. Fluid	Wiper Fluid	Air Filter	Oil Filter	Fuel Filter	Lube	Rotate Tires	Inspect Coolant	Brake Check	Belts & Hoses

Note Repairs/Purchases

Mark C=Check or R=Replace

Mileage/Date	Engine Oil	A.T. Fluid	Wiper Fluid	Air Filter	Oil Filter	Fuel Filter	Lube	Rotate Tires	Inspect Coolant	Brake Check	Belts & Hoses

Note Repairs/Purchases

Mark C=Check or R=Replace

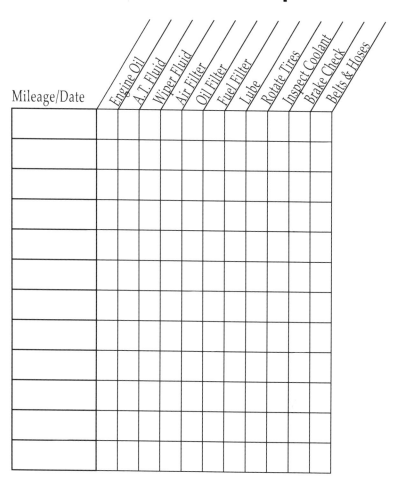

Mileage/Date	Engine Oil	A.T. Fluid	Wiper Fluid	Air Filter	Oil Filter	Fuel Filter	Lube	Rotate Tires	Inspect Coolant	Brake Check	Belts & Hoses

Note Repairs/Purchases

Mark C=Check or R=Replace

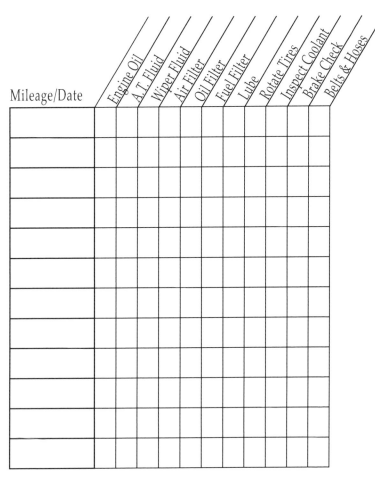

Mileage/Date	Engine Oil	A.T. Fluid	Wiper Fluid	Air Filter	Oil Filter	Fuel Filter	Lube	Rotate Tires	Inspect Coolant	Brake Check	Belts & Hoses

Note Repairs/Purchases

Mark C=Check or R=Replace

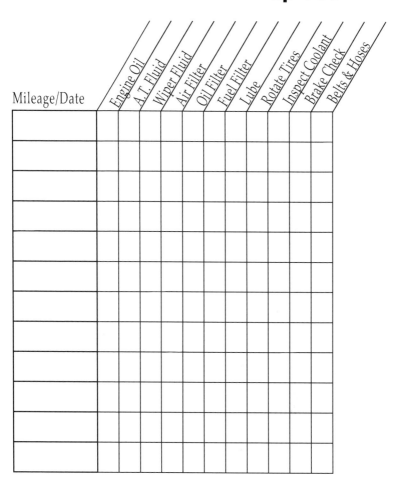

Mileage/Date	Engine Oil	A.T. Fluid	Wiper Fluid	Air Filter	Oil Filter	Fuel Filter	Lube	Rotate Tires	Inspect Coolant	Brake Check	Belts & Hoses

Note Repairs/Purchases

Mark C=Check or R=Replace

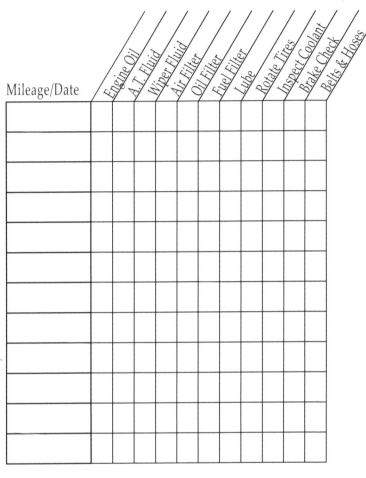

Mileage/Date	Engine Oil	A.T. Fluid	Wiper Fluid	Air Filter	Oil Filter	Fuel Filter	Lube	Rotate Tires	Inspect Coolant	Brake Check	Belts & Hoses

Note Repairs/Purchases

Mark C=Check or R=Replace

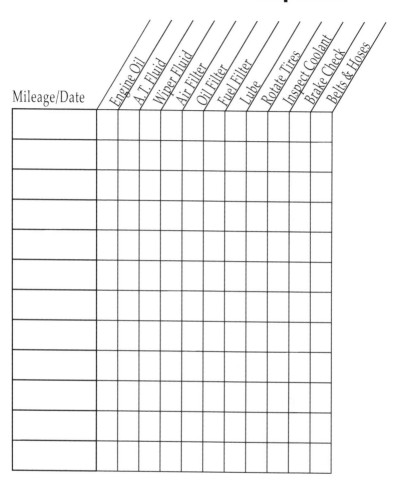

Mileage/Date	Engine Oil	A.T. Fluid	Wiper Fluid	Air Filter	Oil Filter	Fuel Filter	Lube	Rotate Tires	Inspect Coolant	Brake Check	Belts & Hoses

Note Repairs/Purchases

Mark C=Check or R=Replace

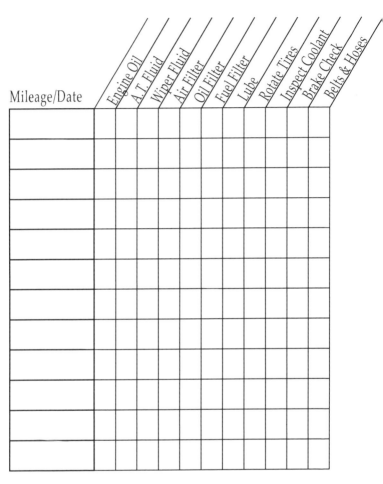

Mileage/Date	Engine Oil	A.T. Fluid	Wiper Fluid	Air Filter	Oil Filter	Fuel Filter	Lube	Rotate Tires	Inspect Coolant	Brake Check	Belts & Hoses

Note Repairs/Purchases

Made in United States
Orlando, FL
28 December 2021